# THE TIGER SHARK

By Sara Green

BELLWETHER MEDIA • MINNEAPOLIS, MN

Jump into the cockpit and
take flight with Pilot books.
Your journey will take you on
high-energy adventures as
you learn about all that is wild,
weird, fascinating, and fun!

This edition first published in 2013 by Bellwether Media, Inc.

No part of this publication may be reproduced in whole or in part without written permission of the publisher.
For information regarding permission, write to Bellwether Media, Inc., Attention: Permissions Department,
5357 Penn Avenue South, Minneapolis, MN 55419.

Library of Congress Cataloging-in-Publication Data

Green, Sara, 1964-
The tiger shark / by Sara Green.
    pages cm. – (Pilot. Shark fact files)
Audience: 8-12.
Summary: "Engaging images accompany information about the tiger shark. The combination of high-interest subject
matter and narrative text is intended for students in grades 3 through 7"–Provided by publisher.
Includes bibliographical references and index.
ISBN 978-1-60014-872-9 (hardcover : alk. paper)
1. Tiger shark–Juvenile literature. I. Title.
QL638.95.C3G75 2013
597.3'4–dc23
                            2012036144

Printed in the United States of America, North Mankato, MN.

# TABLE OF CONTENTS

# TIGER SHARK
## IDENTIFIED

A surfer paddles into the ocean off the coast of Hawaii. His foot dangles in the cool water as he waits for a giant wave to ride to shore. Suddenly a long, pointed fin appears ahead of him. He quickly pulls his foot out of the water. A large shark with a blunt nose swims beneath him. Faint black stripes line its gray back. It's a tiger shark! This is one of the largest, most dangerous sharks in the ocean. The surfer breathes a sigh of relief when the tiger shark swims away. Then he quickly paddles back to shore. There will be no surfing today!

The tiger shark gets its name from the spots and stripes on its gray body. Its belly is yellowish white in color. This countershading allows the shark to blend in with the colors of the ocean and sneak up on prey. The tiger shark averages 10 to 14 feet (3 to 4.3 meters) in length and weighs up to 1,400 pounds (635 kilograms). The largest tiger sharks grow to be more than 20 feet (6.1 meters) long and can weigh nearly 2,000 pounds (907 kilograms).

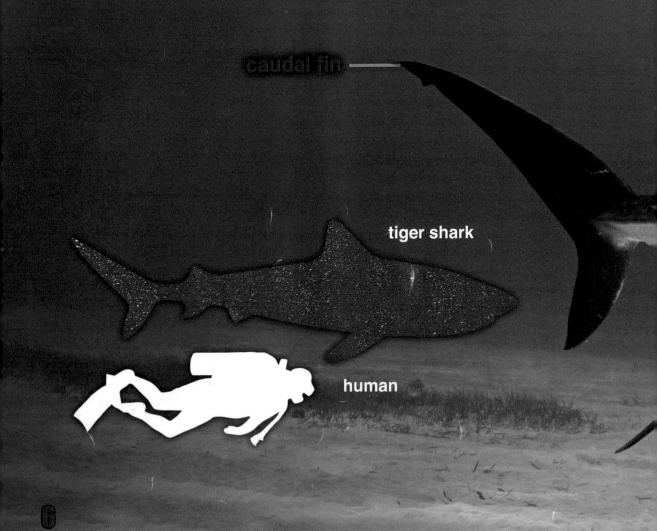

caudal fin

tiger shark

human

The tiger shark's skeleton is made of cartilage. This light, flexible tissue allows it to move and bend easily. The shark sways its powerful caudal fin to gain speed. The pectoral fins allow it to steer and slow down. The dorsal fins keep the shark upright and balanced.

dorsal fins

pectoral fins

Tiger sharks are found worldwide in temperate and tropical oceans. Their habitat ranges from shallow coastal waters to depths over 1,150 feet (350 meters). Young tiger sharks often inhabit the shallow waters over seagrass beds. There they are safe from larger predators.

Tiger sharks migrate with the seasons to follow prey and give birth to young. They swim in cooler waters during spring and summer. In fall and winter, they travel to warm, tropical waters. Many tiger sharks also migrate between islands to hunt prey.

N

W + E

S

= tiger shark territory

# TIGER SHARK
## TRACKED

Tiger sharks are ovoviviparous. The young grow in eggs inside the mother's body. After 13 to 16 months, the eggs hatch. The mother gives birth to a litter of 10 to 80 live young called pups. They are between 20 and 30 inches (51 and 76 centimeters) long. The pups are independent at birth and able to hunt on their own.

Tiger sharks usually mature between 5 and 10 years old. Females then give birth to litters every two to three years. Experts believe tiger sharks may live 30 years or more.

## BUILT-IN CAMOUFLAGE

Young tiger sharks have bold black spots and stripes. These markings blend in with the shadows in shallow water. They make the sharks difficult to spot from the surface.

**TRASH BUFFET**

Tiger sharks have been known to eat some unusual items. Scientists have found antlers, raincoats, license plates, and old tires in their stomachs!

Tiger sharks are aggressive apex predators with huge appetites. They have rows of sharp, serrated teeth that curve inward to trap prey. During the day, tiger sharks often hunt alone in deep waters. At night they move closer to shore. Some sharks travel up to 50 miles (80 kilometers) each day to find food. Tiger sharks will eat almost anything. Their favorite prey includes sea turtles, seals, stingrays, crabs, and other sharks.

Large eyes allow tiger sharks to see prey in dim light. They can follow a scent trail to its source with their nostrils. They also have an excellent sense of hearing. The ampullae of Lorenzini are tiny pores around the shark's snout. These sense the electric fields of nearby animals. The lateral lines on the sides of the body sense the movement of prey in the water.

14

The tiger shark is one of the top three most dangerous sharks in the world. Tiger sharks have attacked about 100 people. At least 30 of them were killed. Many attacks occur because tiger sharks and people swim in the same waters. Tiger sharks mistake people for sea turtles and other favorite prey. Most often, the sharks take a bite and swim away. These attacks cause serious injury, but most are not deadly.

## OVERCOMING THE ODDS

In 2003, thirteen-year-old Bethany Hamilton was surfing off the coast of Hawaii when a tiger shark bit off her left arm. Bethany survived and later taught herself to surf with one arm.

Tiger sharks are important to their ocean habitats. They keep prey populations from growing too large. They eat sick, weak, and slow prey. However, people often fear sharks so much that they prefer to see them dead. In the 1960s and 1970s, the state of Hawaii attempted to rid their coastlines of tiger sharks. Officials thought that killing these sharks would protect people from attacks.

Today, scientists know that this practice is not helpful. It is difficult to single out the sharks that attack people, so many innocent sharks are killed. Instead, people must learn to use caution when they swim in tiger shark territory.

People continue to hunt tiger sharks for their body parts. Their large dorsal fins are used to make shark fin soup. This is a popular food in some Asian countries. The tiger shark's tough skin is used to make leather. The liver is used for its oil.

Tiger sharks are also popular game fish. Sport fishers enjoy the challenge of catching this large, dangerous shark. Many tiger sharks are also caught as bycatch in nets and on lines meant for other fish. For these reasons, the tiger shark has been listed as near threatened by the International Union for Conservation of Nature (IUCN).

# SHARK BRIEF

**Common Name:** Tiger Shark

**Also Known As:** Wastebasket of the Sea

**Claim to Fame:** Stomach often contains garbage

**Hot Spots:**
The Bahamas
Caribbean Sea
Pacific Islands

**Life Span:** 30 years or more

**Current Status:** Near Threatened (IUCN)

EXTINCT

EXTINCT IN THE WILD

CRITICALLY ENDANGERED

ENDANGERED

VULNERABLE

NEAR THREATENED

LEAST CONCERN

Scientists know a lot about tiger sharks, but many questions remain about how these fierce predators live. Researchers track tiger sharks to gather more information about their travel patterns. They discover where tiger sharks hunt, find mates, and give birth. This information helps researchers create plans that protect tiger shark habitats. It can also teach people where to avoid fishing for tiger sharks. With this help, the striped shark with the unending appetite has a bright future!

# GLOSSARY

**ampullae of Lorenzini**—a network of tiny jelly-filled sacs around a shark's snout; the jelly is sensitive to the electric fields of nearby prey.

**apex predators**—predators that are not hunted by any other animal

**bycatch**—animals that are accidentally caught with fishing nets or lines

**cartilage**—flexible connective tissue that makes up a shark's skeleton

**caudal fin**—the tail fin of a fish

**countershading**—coloring that helps camouflage an animal; fish with countershading have pale bellies and dark backs.

**dorsal fins**—the fins on the back of a fish

**electric fields**—waves of electricity created by movement; every living being has an electric field.

**game fish**—fish caught for sport

**lateral lines**—a system of tubes beneath a shark's skin that helps it detect changes in water pressure

**mature**—to become old enough to reproduce

**migrate**—to travel from one place to another, often with the seasons

**near threatened**—could soon be at risk of becoming endangered

**ovoviviparous**—producing young that develop in eggs inside the body; ovoviviparous animals give birth to live young.

**pectoral fins**—a pair of fins that extend from each side of a fish's body

**seagrass beds**—large areas of grass-like plants that grow in shallow coastal waters

**serrated**—having a jagged edge

**temperate**—neither too warm nor too cold

# TO LEARN MORE

## At the Library

Lewis, Brenda Ralph. *Sharks*. Milwaukee, Wis.: Gareth Stevens Pub., 2006.

Mathea, Heidi. *Tiger Sharks*. Edina, Minn.: ABDO Pub., 2011.

Nuzzolo, Deborah. *Tiger Shark*. Mankato, Minn.: Capstone Press, 2011.

## On the Web

Learning more about tiger sharks is as easy as 1, 2, 3.

1. Go to www.factsurfer.com.

2. Enter "tiger sharks" into the search box.

3. Click the "Surf" button and you will see a list of related Web sites.

With factsurfer.com, finding more information is just a click away.

# INDEX

The images in this book are reproduced through the courtesy of: Scott Sansenbach –
Sansenbach Marine Photo/Getty Images, front cover, p. 21; A Cotton Photo, pp. 4-5;
auremar, pp. 4-5 (top); Pacific Stock – Design Pics/SuperStock, pp. 6-7; Masa Ushioda/
WaterF/Agefotostock, pp. 8-9; Andre Seale/VWPics/SuperStock, pp. 10-11; Image Source/
Getty Images, pp. 12-13; spaceshark, p. 14; Gustavo Miguel Fernandes, p. 15; Dr. James P.
McVey, NOAA Sea Grant Program, p. 16; NaturePL/SuperStock, p. 17; Jeffrey L. Rotman/
Getty Images, pp. 18-19.